SHE CHASING HIRAETH

SANSKRITI BHARDWAJ

ISBN 979-888591523-6

I, as the author of "**She Chasing Hiraeth**",

dedicate this book to

Love and womankind.

Women of all shades, shapes, and types

Powerful women,

Beautiful women.

And the mighty emotion of Love.

Contents

Contents

Contents

Contents

She Chasing Hiraeth

-Sanskriti Bhardwaj

Acknowledgements

This book taught me the worth of being a woman. The strength I carry and the massive love I serve to the people around me as a female.

I would love to challenge myself to the extremes and continue creating compositions of Victory and Power. I am delighted to end this beautiful creation of mine and submit it to all my dear readers with felicity and pride. I would extend my gratitude to my parents, Mr. Hemant Kumar Jha and Mrs. Rina Jha for constantly supporting and cherishing me as their daughter . I would like to thank Miss. Yashika Karamchandani wholeheartedly for being kind enough to be by my side and helping me in the publishing process

As a matter of fact, **"She Chasing Hiraeth"** will be an absolute inspiration to my feminism and I will love it with all my substance. I hope and pray that the readers feel the very same way I want them to feel after reading each piece in particular.

It was an honor being able to write another book in a short period of time after **"Vaitarni"**. I will continue expressing myself wholeheartedly through more books as possible.

Thank you again.

Regards

Sanskriti Bhardwaj .

About The Author

Sanskriti Bhardwaj , the author of "Vaitarni" , is a young writing enthusiast from the city of Darbhanga , Bihar . She is a student chasing her dreams along with the burning passion towards art and literature . She loves to read and pen down her emotions in form of poetry . In her opinion , nothing is more superior than the power to express yourself .

Sanskriti loves to read . Having a deep interest in British classics , she spends her time in solitude with books as her best companions . As an ambivert writer , she finds a beam of hope radiating from the famous compositions of Jane Austen , Thomas Hardy , William Shakespeare , Wordsworth , Bronte sisters and others . Reading novels and writing poems are her favourite things to do .

Art is her home . She loves playing with colours and creating joy . For her , Art is the solution to all her problems . It is like a therapy to soothe her anxiety . Art liberates her soul . Be it water colours or oil pastels , markers or acrylics or even a piece of charcoal is all what she needs to lift her mood . She has won several awards for her paintings . She expresses her heart through abstract paintings with women protagonists .

"She Chasing Hiraeth" is her second solo book and the first in English language . "Vaitarni" , her first solo book won loads of appreciation from the readers . Sanskriti has been a part of multiple anthologies . Her work has been published in several books like – The Buried Tales , Women not Weak , Candle , The Saga of Love ,

Life is a Game , Gehraiyaan , The Ones Behind The Bars , Fog in the Hollow and many more as a coauthor . She has also compiled two anthologies , Wabi-Sabi and Bitter and Sweet . The front cover of Wabi-Sabi has been hand painted by Sanskriti .

As a person , Sanskriti is reserved and ambivert . She doesn't prefers the company of people much . Her interests are vintage . Her parents provided her moral support and strength to perform well in adversities . She got her inspiration in writing as an inheritance from her mother who shares the same interests as her . Sanskriti has an elder sister and a younger brother along with whom she grew up with adoration and love . Last year on her birthday she gifted herself a friend , more of a little sister , a female beagle whom she named "Angelina" and with her she understood the emotions of love and care in proximity .

Sanskriti is a young feminist who loves to express herself through art and poetry . She is cheerful , kind and believes strongly in the power of love . She is a vagabond chasing her Hiraeth by the help of ink and paint .

About The Book

"She Chasing Hiraeth" is a book of dreams and strength . Second book from the author after "Vaitarni" , it is the first in English language . It was a dream come true being able to write this wonderful piece and produce it in front of the readers with great expectations and joy . It was a milestone , crossing which helped me to become more worthy of lifting a pen .

While framing down the verses , I realised the wonder in being a woman . The pride , elegance and strength which flooded my veins by birth which I was far from familiar with . It was like self observation and enlightenment . I became strong and accustomed to my feminity . My inner goddess is obliged to this composition .

The cover of the book highlights the name of the book in bold . Designed by me , the cover is conveying vintage vibes . I depicted myself on the front and back cover as the protagonist chasing her **Hiraeth** . The aesthetic of this book is feminine vintage and the wilted shades of colours help the theme to pop out more . On the back cover , I could be seen pleating my hair strands into a bundle as I wish to collect all the chaos of my life into something sort of strength .

The book is however raw and stimulating . The name of book is itself appealing . The use of the word Hiraeth, literally meaning homesickness for a home you never had , makes the title lively and emotional . I loved how the whole composition took a vulnerable form due to its title although the poetry in there is all about the massive strength a woman carries in herself and all the adversities she has to face in her life . This book brings out the poignant side of being a female along with love , power and sacrifice as vital emotions .

In my opinion , "She Chasing Hiraeth" is my capsule of fighting the distress and misery I face being a woman . Each and every poem inside ignites my feminism and helps me peer deep into my soul . As I read aloud this book , all I am left with is inspiration and solidity . It was a kind and empowering decision of my life when I penned down this wonderful book.

1. Poem 1

There were some magicians
Thirsting over
The kind of magic she
Teased while her hair
Twined along with shallow
Tides of lust and a
Thousand reasons for death
Together creating hallucinations for
Them to plunder all kinds of sinful
Thoughts of pleasure and
Taming their monsters , feeding them
Tulips and wine
Tasting their guilts and
Taking all smokes of
Tiresome energy which cannot be gulped
Through
Two or four of nostrils .
The black magic on which she danced
Threw glimpses of her dark sanity
To and fro all the magicians hovered
Trying chances to steal her possessions .
There she stood

Talking with her darlings and protecting
The kingdom of magic she carried in her smallness .

2. Poem 2

She inhales vivid shades of lavender
Far stretched the fields of drunk flowers
Resting over her shoulders
Pouring blush of random hues
And giving birth to sunshine
Few gemstones fall down
Through her eyes crossing dimples
And a sharp chin on their way down
Her breasts and belly and ginger thighs
Lavender bedspread and lavender scent
She was craving the fiction and poetry
Juices that melt from the lavender loosely .

3. Poem 3

All her futile attempts of channelizing
Her feminity leaving behind
Traces of agony and inferiority
Gathered in her womb
Exhausted yet straining her strength
To the core of the will .
She desperately criticizes her shadow
For not leaving her alone when she
Begs for mercy of some self time .
She wears nail polish , and ties all her hair in
A ponytail , carries herself over high heels
Five inches raising her phobia of reputation
Fighting a place , a fist sized sky over her
Burdened shoulders .
She cooked meals and added salt as per their taste
She never was strong
They didn't let her be one
Strong woman .

4. Poem 4

There have been nights where I never felt
Skin or bones
All you made me feel was something
Not at all humanly
Were those nights mirage,
A total falsehood?
Or there existed a "heaven"
Under my white sheets
Into your pit of embrace !

5. Poem 5

A billion heads and I fell asleep on your shoulder
Dreaming of good times and home to my vagabond heart .

6. Poem 6

Mom,

I raped a girl.

And I am not scared, I did it for fun.

Yes, her body was a delight

And I feasted on her curves while she laid

Half lifeless and full mute

She was so weak and terrified

It made me happy to bully her dignity.

I squeezed her breasts with my manly palm

Engulfing that woman into my fist

As she needed to be controlled and taught a lesson

I kicked and thrashed her, clenching her from hair

Plucked out her nails,

Those red nail polish were hurting my eyes.

Tore her dress, very short, a sign that she wanted me

She wanted a man shoved into her

And what an act she played!

Crying and sobbing and begging and saying NO

Such a bitch.

Mom, as a son, I always make you proud

And this Christmas,

I hope you would buy me the latest phone .

7. Poem 7

She wore Petrichor as her perfume.

8. Poem 8

It was that part of month
When red wild roses fell down
From her panties
The hundred shades of lipsticks of Red
That she owned
Were thus , how she differentiated the hues .

9. Poem 9

Each night,
When the town succumbs to sleep
And the streetlight faints, dim
The white curtains from the old box windows of houses
Stop dancing with the wind and
Wrap the room in silence
The silhouette of the dreams of wives and daughters
Were painted on the silver lines bordering the moon
Each night, when rebellious women
Hover around the outskirts of the town
Creating graffiti on the walls of gloomy streets
And kissing under Venus shining overhead
'The moon and her girlfriends'
Raise a toast to
Feminity.
Drunk and drenched in freedom
They sing lullabies for the men to sleep
A little longer .

10. Poem 10

She is raging winds of the coasts
where the sun meets the water
and the absolute truth meets falsehood.
She is the koi fish
dancing on a lady's cheeks,
gulping her sickness
and playing with the water
under her eye bags.
She is blazing northern lights
of reds and greens and purples enveloping the darkest dreams
of the shivering nights.
Debussy's Clair de Lune
may lead you to her.

11. Poem 11

She tears her soul everyday .
Everyday ,
While she smiles
She is sick inside .
Fighting thousand interrogations
And staring eyes .
She craves for a shoulder
Or a cosy lap .
She is homesick
For a home she never had !

12. Poem 12

Her lips of riots
And her waist disciplined by the corset
The perfect height
The perfect gowns of finest muslin
Layers and layers to obstruct
What a raging storm is within
Her untamed hair put into styles
Clutched under pins and bands
Married to dignified men
And touched by all decent hands
All possible methods of domesticating
The mind and will , born to run through the meadows
Fight wars , rule nations , create art , write the greatest poems
Speak , laugh , eat , love and die free .

13. Poem 13

Some wild metaphors fell down
From in between her words
The death she personified
Had layers of foundations
And concealers to hide all those darkest circles
When she sang
The poems shivered
And when she danced naked
What a sight of strength and beauty
She painted deadly strokes
With her bruised fingers oozing elixir
Her body was marvellous
And her heart made of mountains
She was powerful
She carried art in her womb for billions of years
She was an art herself.

14. Poem 14

She plays Für Elise
On the funeral of her expectations .
Her love letters flew out of the car
After creating havoc of agony and nostalgia
And the scent of writhed rose petals
Suffocated her nostrils .
She wiped the wet mess on her cheeks
And accelerated down the dead end .
Für Elise was played
On her funeral
While she rested in peace
Enjoying her favourite classic
Torment free .

15. Poem 15

Breasts and Vaginas
Filled the voids
Of oceans
Manufacturing mammoth feminity
Tender fingers
With great strength .
Started climbing mountains
And breathing in hurricanes .
Breasts and Vaginas
Leaked fragrances of
Unorthodox and peaceful wills
Producing hope and women
Grace and gratitude
Unfiltered and raw
Started milking their souls
Feeding new born men with benevolence .

16. Poem 16

Mighty
Mothers
Making
Miracles

17. Poem 17

Dancing around campfire
And villianizing her existence
Ineffable dark expressions
Which hovered around her larynx
Pushing out squeaks to be heard
She smiled in her red wine gulps
Reasoning with distress flooding her veins
Popping out drama
Pumping in sobs
She felt the fever from the fire
Observing her figure into the
Flames performing ballet
She jumped into the fire
After drinking kerosene .

18. Poem 18

No words could envelope
Her naked dead body
The pit of her stomach craved
Love .
Her brown body with patches of trauma
Justifying the hatred they had for her
Her words poisoned their ego
They tried to mute her , pulled her tongue out
Snapped both of her jaws .
She was in pain
There was a haemorrhage within her soul
She cried , shouted , moaned
As if thunder jolted in her lungs .
She was fed to anxiety
They made her a victim .
She was once a fighter .

19. Poem 19

Touch me not
Dear stranger ,
Don't loot my sanity
Don't tease my oestrogen !

20. Poem 20

Cry baby
You cry too much
They conquer your joy
You try too much
You tore yourself up
Into shreds
Cry baby
Your sour head .
Your deadly guilt
Your dead dreams
Cry baby
With broken wings
Tattoo on your ankle
A sign infinite
They make you cry
Red purple sight
Cry baby
Don't you stop crying
They will burden your will
Never stop sighing .

21. Poem 21

Let me sing the agony
Of skies under thunder wars
Let me memorize the last sigh
Your air pumped filled my lungs
Let me tremble under the curse
Of serpents and fox.
Let us meet on the day
After the equinox .

22. Poem 22

The next time , I sleep
I wish to be enveloped by
Golden nightmares .
The far seeming apocalypse
Fluttering wings
Like a butterfly
Dancing with the breeze
And sucking nectar
Or lives .
The crow from the graveyard
Making a nest on my dreams
Fetching distant memories
Of separation and anxiety
Creating catastrophe
Inside my reckless head .
People , with unfaithful touch
Pleasing me with artificial smiles
Kissing my cheeks with blue and
Purple poison tinted lips .
Heavily positioning their useless opinions
In the circumference of my
Dilemma .

23. Poem 23

Beautiful faces
And ugly temptations
Luxurious bags
And nilpossessions
Those culprit hands of
Women with wonderful sins
Carving headlines
gathering fame
Seeking power , well they are
Fragmented from inside out .
Women with deceiving smiles
Cry whole night
As their mascara seeps down lashes
Creating tsunami of blackness and broken strength
Such women wear appealing styles
Carry their feminism along
Like they carry lipsticks in their purse .

24. Poem 24

Hypnotism is her side business.

25. Poem 25

When she speaks
They scrape out her tongue
When she is mute
They celebrate .
When she stands
They pull her down
When she falls
They crush her jubilantly .

26. Poem 26

It was a winter night
People slept cosily
She was raped and thrown
Naked on the street .

27. Poem 27

She drank five and a half
Milky ways
Sucked all the nebulas
Filled her voids with
Comets
The colour of her eyeball
Resembled that of black holes
Starlight gleamed
Over her brown tainted skin
She was the woman of universe
With mighty will
And deeply concealed secrets .
With a pinch of dust from space and time
Women revive and retain .

28. Poem 28

Disease gulped her stomach
Agony danced her way
She crouched and called
Her distress was never harnessed
There she stood
In the middle of the world
With her wounds being showcased and applauded
Where people rushed and hovered
With fists full of salt
To rub her bruises
And envelope her torment .
No one discovered
That she was meek .
She loved humanity
But feared humans for sure .

29. Poem 29

Under the stampede of thoughts
Her mouth laid vulgar
Stealing curses and broken abuses
A murmur was heard
From the corner of the room
Hush , Hush !
Chaos paved his way
As children slept in the laps of
Mothers , midnight
On tip toes , she moved out
With loads on her backbone and
Bills to pay
She mocked those mouths
Once filthy who said
She ran across the streets
Not running errands this time
Leaping the signals and blazing starlight
Went on a mission to carry her head
Out in front , all straight , with dignity
She sprinkled wisdom on the bushes across the pavement
Kissed the wild flowers on the cracked walls
Was , it morning already ?

She had to finish the chores , Alas !

30. Poem 30

There had been dust on the pages
And on the shelves
The worms had eaten all the meaningful words
And puked nothingness on the coarse surface
Of wisdom and willingness .
The protagonist still alive , combed her hair every evening on the
balcony.

31. Poem 31

Smart women with unique individuality
Persistent and persuasive
Walk alone
However , walk alone .

32. Poem 32

She saw degradation cascading
Down her heels
Making her trip and stumble .
She clutched her fist
And her footsteps revolved
Enveloping her existence
Within a bottle of wine .
What made her blown away ?
What made her temptations kiss
The crumbs of ignition .
What made her ego sinister ?

33. Poem 33

Dwelling frozen and lifeless
Begging for a duplicatesting
Stood her melancholy
Dancing before the bridge .
As cheaters cheated
And raindrops settled
Eloped her agony
Along the breeze .
Envy her
Capture all the volume
Carry her frame
Let the bullet ease .
Culprit of her sins
An oath to reciprocate
She hurried and confessed
Crossing fine fire lease .

34. Poem 34

There have been days
She slept naked
With her anxiety
Having a wholesome meal .
She crawled under the bedspread
Hid her lungs
Thorns and roses
Giggling bed bugs .
What a scene
What a turmoil
What a meaningless poetry !
She carved herself a sculpture
To caress her during sleep .
Nightmares and sunshine
Violet and cheese
She wailed fragments of lies
A promise to keep .

35. Poem 35

Oh mighty ,
Virago !
Enlighten me
Feed me power
Strengthen me .
Fill my voids with dare
Teach me to fight
Distress drinking my tear
Aggression and fuel is what I need
End my fear .
War is what I preach
Power flew me here .

36. Poem 36

Women are wayfarers .

37. Poem 37

A mug of alcohol
A bundle of dreams
Inside her pocket
Six coins and a seed
Of dandelion
Trying hard to escape
The threads of foreign thoughts
Sew agony and suffering
Her hopes were bouncing
And sliding over the
Fractals of euphoria .
She pondered upon
The use of six coins
After fighting the inertia !

38. Poem 38

They had claws and wings
And tempest in their hearts
They giggled beheld energies
And crossed mammoth paths .

39. Poem 39

Ladies with breasts
Of sizes of melons and peas
With brutal sacrifices
And ocean of feels .
Ladies with unconditional
Love and consideration
Protecting men and children
Pride of nation .
Ladies with wisdom
Like sages and philosophers
Enlightening families
And numerous generations .

40. Poem 40

Is your menstrual painful ?
Don't you stop working !

41. Poem 41

Away from the dimensions
Of space and time
Thrives a no lesser lonely
Soul
Drinking sips of
Unspoken words
Smelling like roses crippled
And writhed in between the pages
Of love stories from ages
Reciprocates and surpasses
Avoiding gazes of villains
How awkwardly yet with a handful of grace
The soul prays
Meddling life with ease
The life, of someone deceased .

42. Poem 42

She infuses her milk
With blood and tears
As the petite young one
Sucks on her body
Quenching thirst and hunger .
She pours strength and manhood
Into each and every vein
Like nectar
Lying supine on the yards of
Struggles and bitterness in the near future
She conveys her glory and magnificence
Without uttering a single sound
Without getting a praise for her work
Without expecting applaud
She is a mother , a selfless creature indeed .

43. Poem 43

Women are born wicked and bold .
Women carry elegance on
The tip of their tongue
Women create history
History itself is a woman
A woman with pride
And glory
Ages to command
And congratulate the
Trace of space of goodness
Women are warriors
They fight with thunderous strength
Women are peacekeepers
They boil peace in a saucepan
And serve it hot to the family
And society and the world .
Women distort themselves
In the kitchens-offices-fields
In front of sparkling cameras and
Gazing eyes
Women are artworks
We all are refugees

Welcomed heartedly by womankind .

44. Poem 44

She has seen carvings and illustrations
Paintings and compositions
Of the masters
With perfection and grandeur
Feeding fuel of paints
Splashes and drops
Paintbrushes speaking the dialects of
Memories and the good old days
The fragrance of paintings
With women of all shapes and styles
Sent her chills .
As if she wanted , wished to
Recreate those masterpieces
She imagined herself as the heroines
She saw a reflection of herself in the eyes of
Venus , Mona Lisa , girl with the pearl
And all the beautiful women
Hung on the walls of art museums for centuries and decades
Or in the crumbled pages of a diary
She saw herself as an art .
She began to love herself and the world .

45. Poem 45

The mirror on the wall
Hid hundreds of her faces
While she put on a fake smile
And carried layers of hoax
The mirror filled all her flaws
And unpleasant into itself
Showing her the differing .
She loved her mirror whole heartedly
Until one miserable day
She saw herself in someone's eyes
Her perfect impression of herself was ruined
She was ugly and defeated
She was scared of herself .
Indeed she was ugly as they used to mock her .

46. Poem 46

Oh her beautiful splendid face !
Worth more than diamonds and gems
Like the divinity of angels from heaven
Ineffable absolutely .
Chocolate eyes like burnt black magic
Peering into the soul
Hair bundles hanging down the waist
And the waist like that of a serpent dancing
Her cheekbones recited poetry
And she was like a painting or a sculpture .
She was distorted after a splash of acid
Dissolved with just half a bottle
She was still beautiful
But who had the eyes to acknowledge .
Her face was made a matter of discussions and mere gossips
Her body was mocked for the way it deformed
After surgeries multiple times
Her eyes lost hope and all the gleam
Dust accumulated on her cheeks and nose bridge
Her waist was tired of lifting the weight of her burnt face
She was burnt and
Was in pain .

47. Poem 47

People visited her grave
After brutally murdering her hopes .

48. Poem 48

Hands , held the malicious termite
Hands , fought with pens and swords
Hands , led the mankind
Hands , created and presented .
Her hands were wonderful .

49. Poem 49

somewhere ,
sometime .
in the tragedy of hers ,
you will always be found .
in her rhymes and art ,
you will always exist .

50. Poem 50

If tears left scars

Nobody ever cried .

If blood turned black

Nobody ever sighed

"I will make you feel special "

Was a promise to be broken

Each day I wrestle

with guilt mere spoken .

You leave a hole

It aches there

In the deepest of this soul

It lacks care

If nobody is mine

Where I belong to ?

Nothing left as time

What I shouldn't , what you should.

Sleep vs death

Which one should I choose

My demons are craving dark

How to let them loose ?

If tears left scars then

I will cry till doom .

51. Poem 51

Every time
When there is a part of me
escaping
a part of me pretending
I feel illusion.
A never ending saga of
trust and dedication
of sorrow and guilt
shielding my existence.
I feel safer when I am lost
This world is bubble
and so truthful is my
short termed yet vivid
misconception.
Love is permanent
though only myth
yet it assures me of my being .

52. Poem 52

Bottle her teardrops

And there will be a new ocean on the world map .

53. Poem 53

There stands always an equilibrium
between heart and the emotional constituents
which are antagonistic yet allied .
The heart wants love , hope , felicity and likeness
But all what it is left with are mere feelings of vanity , hate ,
agony and jealousy .
It seems sadness is more prominent than joy.
So an emotional equilibrium appears
almost an irony or total falsehood to her .
As for her , the world revolves
around the niche of sadness
and it holds supremacy over her puny existence !

54. Poem 54

Only those who caress their own deeds and needs
are the ones truly capable of loving others .
No love is as superior and strong
As the love for oneself .
Love yourself
As you wish to be loved by others .

55. Poem 55

It is one of the several thousand truth
That a manly ego is as fragile as a womanly heart
And the whole universe , with all its vastness ,
However does bends before this truth solely !

56. Poem 56

And she was raped
And what we did
And she was harassed
And what we did
And she was tortured
And what we did
And she died of her pain
And what we did
Well yes , we lit some candles
We led a march
We posted and reposted and liked and commented
She left ...time passed ....we forgot
And she was raped !

57. Poem 57

There were strech marks
On her thighs and belly
Breasts and arms
Carved on her body everywhere
Like the stripes of a tigress
Marching ahead in the jungle
In royalty and with pride .

58. Poem 58

What is it like to be crushed
Everyday by hopeless expectations ?
You won't know — it's suffocating .
cry alone in the shower .
To fade your tears in water
Seeping down your crevices .
But unable to wipe your black within !
Your muted shouts are heard by your loneliness
Who mocks at you thumping both its feet .
You are pierced a hundred million times
All over and again and again
Until you fake a smile and say
I am fine ... It's ok !
You are torn into shreds and fed to anxiety .
You hate yourself for loving
You vanish slowly but nobody notices
And you are clutched from your hair and dragged ruthlessly .
And like a dried flower's petals you writhe away .
Holding beautiful memories of love .
Holding assaults of death and heartache .
Holding emptiness .

59. Poem 59

There is nothing as special
And warm as love she carries in her heart .
People spit on her
Yet she embraces them
As if there is nothing more of love remaining in her .
She is fertile as a forest cover
Green and lush
Life for her is some sort of a strory
And she , a raconteur , very fine at her job .

60. Poem 60

We distant ourselves
From propinquity
After heartaches deserting our peace .
Solitude becomes most respectable
And there is nothing more to desire from others .
We keep hanging there
Accustomed to nothing
We monitor the environment
With lithe ballerinas dancing on tip toes
Without grace , falling on their hips
Breaking bones and tearing ligaments .
We pretend not disliking them
While something in us breaks like those silly bones .
We hold ourselves with elegance
Fighting a safe place
To input some sense into dead brain cells .
We love to play suduko
And fall off ladders , running away from snakes .
We are lost and afraid of
Never to be found by anyone again .

61. Poem 61

She sings lullaby
For the children to sleep
While father is smoking cigarettes
And clashing glasses of whiskey .
She lifts babies in her arm
And kisses away their teary eyes
Placing a tika on their forehead
Protecting them from evil sights .

62. Poem 62

Sisters and daughters and mothers and wives
Are pristine lakes of love
The purest emotions flow in their veins
As they are balms on aches
They are strong and worthy
They are capable of love .

63. Poem 63

He was a panacea to her
She was a mess in perfect skin .

64. Poem 64

I had a dream
The silhoutte of which still lingers
On the nerves of my mind.
I felt you close to my existence
Peering into my gaze
The taste of you filled my tongue with elixir .
It was a holy dream .
The tryst was inexpressible
I wished to never wake up
Later in my dream
You broke me
And my dream broke like
The shattered mirror on my dressing table .
Now it ended as something more of reality
Something acceptable
Something far from fallacy .

65. Poem 65

Every day is a new struggle
The beginning is some angst
The end is misery.
When you shed your wings
Like hair falling off
From a cancer patient's body.
I am stuck in the middle of
Nowhere
Trusting in myths leads to disaster.
I gulp tears and laugh shamelessly
Creating havoc
I am gullible, oh goodness!

66. Poem 66

In the nadir of my thirst
Lied a woman
Such a liar she was .
In the mirror , i saw a hunter
With ego as long as my tongue
Sharping and barking
Blowing the silence off of their lips
She was short sighted
She couldn't see future
She only could read and write and play
Music bursted her ears
She was insulted and submerged into
Sweats and blood
After sex
She was harnessed
Like petrol , she burnt
A coward fuel !

67. Poem 67

What shines behind the small windmill in the middles of woods
Was a sumptuous bungalow
A lady died there everyday
Starving to death , as
There was nothing to have
Except diamonds and gems and
A scintilla of lonliness .

68. Poem 68

She danced on ice
Gleamed like sun
For six months straight
She lusted the warmth
For the next six
She lived on gasoline.
Loving the shades of glazing light
Hurriedly moving through the sky
Creeping inwards
Crawling out
Creating wonders in front of ours'
Heart and sight
Beauty and amazement
Drooled down the sky
Watching the Aurora Borealis
Was on her bucket list .

69. Poem 69

They made her inure to the depth of harshness
And toxic sights .
She grew up hovering
Over the crazy mindset of society .
She feared eyes and tongues the most
Reserved to herself
There was not a world for her
Other than books
Like novels a home to
Her distressed heart
She was a settled nomad
Quenching her need
With helium balloons
And stories
Of romances and adventures
Of strong bold women .

70. Poem 70

The zillion questions wailing behind
My consciousness
Tormenting me without skipping even the smallest chance
Made me realise
How minute I am
How gigantic is the universe .
The silliest question out of all
Is that "Who am I?"
Thankfully , I ate up all the words
And mumbled to myself
"you are nothing yet everything"
Senselessly !

71. Poem 71

Love seldom lets people live .

72. Poem 72

What are conclusions ?
The punctured opinions
Made into axioms after irrational conversations .
Like drunk people
Rebel in intoxication .
What are tantrums ?
The relevant response from a woman
After child birth or just mere
Menstruation
While she hesitantly squeaks for a day off .

73. Poem 73

The ashtray filled up with pink liquid
Oozing out of my nostrils
I stare at my translucent hands
And observe how the essence of smoke
Dances in my bloodstream
My pink cigarettes are delicious
As I made them with my pastel nightmares .

74. Poem 74

Some dreams are hopeless
Mine are too
I invite them to stay over
And celebrate
Gallons of alcohol
To set the limits free
And to bathe into
Hopelessness
Again and again
Like abandoned life
Ripped off by a ghost
Haphazardly after 2:00 a.m.
Dreams are fragments of
Untouched virgin thoughts
Relentlessly sinking into
Captivity .
Someone , wake me up
Dreams are killing me .
Sweet Poison !

75. Poem 75

Unbroken promises are
The most honest myths .
Promises are bubbles
Short living .

76. Poem 76

She had a sugar rush
Feeding on lime .
Caressed the creased
Be kind .
Gunpowder and paint drops
Mixing with time .
Baby , you were just pretending
What a crime !

77. Poem 77

I never went to the beach
Pa , didn't teach me to swim
I never laid back on the sand
And felt alive in dead skin
I never trusted the waves
I never tried to sink
The echo of confessions
Settled on the brink
I held all my anger
Got no time to think
Lost behind the shallow
Sunset on my kink .

78. Poem 78

Pink lips
Peach cheeks
Holy , she was an angel
Walking on the rainbow
And enchanting everyone
Her honey smile
Made me ponder
What an artist god was !
She was something to
I would surrender .

79. Poem 79

I could find heaven
In her streetlight eyes
Where the city dust
Collapsed
Leaving golden residue .
Women of all shades and sizes
With double eyelids or almond eyes
Marigold bodies
Carried a part of heaven in them .
They passed on repeatedly
This heritage
To their daughters and theirs .
The power to create magic
Hold black magic in eyes .

80. Poem 80

As I rub my eyes
Experiencing a saga of
Phosphenes
A smoke emerges in front of me
Taking the live form
Of my inner goddess
All I am left with is
A bucket of amazement
Lifting my chin upwards , I questioned her
How am I doing as a woman ?
She claimed , advancing towards me
"You are a strong woman
You are beautiful
You are worthy of it !"
Suddenly , I opened my eyes
And in front of me
Was someone ironical , a meek , frightened woman
Fighting each day
With herself in this cruel world .

81. Poem 81

I feed my soul some burnt ash
of vivid expectations
and conjuring memories
Then suck some wisdom
of decaying crafts
to satisfy the cravings
I cry and repent and then repeat
all trials go in vain
And if I try to pull my limits
I succumb to my guilty pleasures again
When roses die and violets vanish
into the cruel disastrous hope
I linger on to my
one and only
Filthy , melting , tempting soul .

82. Poem 82

Dear men,

I am weak and I cry often .

I am easy to be slaughtered and suppressed .

I am fragile .

My dignity can be snatched away anytime you desire

My face can be dissolved by acid

Or my head can be shaved

My dreams , hopes and freedom can be murdered ruthlessly .

You can treat me anyhow you want

God made you demonic and oppressive by nature

Wrath flows in your hormones

Your penis is the representation of superiority and strength

Your existence depends on your masculinity

I am just puny creature with a body to satisfy your thirst and

needs

I am just a "Mighty" woman who is quite

I conceived the world in my womb for a billion years Gave birth

to the entire mankind

God knows himself – "He is a Her" !

83. Poem 83

I took a white flower in my hand
And pearly tears dried
Everything paused for a whole second
When I gave up on fake smiles
I plucked all its petals
And saddened
Remember his cold heart
Remembered his pretty little lies
I sobbed and then smiled
That's what the flower taught .
Holding the pieces in my hands
Like I hold painful magic in my eyes
Whispered to myself
" You are powerful
But it's ok to cry ."

84. Poem 84

You and your promises are a total falsehood.
Your going away haunts me
every day I try to escape this universe With all my strength
Every day the gravity of separation
pulls me back into its wilderness.
I am exhausted. Shall I still wait for you?
Millions of unanswered prayers shatter my faith every day.
The sun never sets on my balcony these days
Red wine tastes salty.
The music is a noise now.
I feel something pumping life in me
My heart is the one little proof I am here.
My chest somehow feels hollow without your heart in me.
Everyday appears to be page of a horror novel.
Your going away is a trauma.
Anxiety is at its peak. I am dying each day a little.
Someone, save me!

85. Poem 85

I scorned at the woman in mirror
She stood tall and her fragile figure
caressed her deadly soul
How come no one saw the poison in her head except me.
I threw my sight away in disdain.
She was powerful and manipulating but I was not.
As I flushed with guilt, my purple lungs sucked in misery
slowly, slowly, slowly
The black hole inside the mirror Sucked all my existence
All I could do was attempt some useless
resistance. Yes, resistance.
I thought of the people again.
They mocked me, the humiliation
The discomfort came dancing before my eyes.
I rushed to the bed and dived in the sheets
They contained my scent and agony
My head showcased me past
haunting memories of past …
Can I resist myself? Can I live?
I closed my sore eyes trying to escape all this
Horror evaporated.
My inside fought a war that night.

There was blood and death
There was gloom and hatred.
I woke up after killing my dreams
My hands soaked in red and my head celebrated its victory
She won… or did she?
Someone there? Marks on my chest
peeling the skin of my breasts and down my thighs
told stories of darker nights
Pain was normal
Hopeless!
Angels had a campfire near my bedpost.
I was shackled and then burnt over the firewood.
My heart oozed black, And they tasted it.
This was how, The angels turned devil.
I was their mother.
The depth of my chaos had no end.
The seven sins kissed my feet each night
I was the woman in the mirror.
I was powerful once.

86. Poem 86

Vivid and excruciating,
A burning hell in my mouth,
I can taste agony and guilt,
People, I am a misfit,
People, let me breathe at least,
Black gulp of liberation,
Or fringes of feels,
Some far away in Eden,
My expectation feeds,
Fuel and fire, death and fury,
Rumours rush and ruckus hurry,
I am building a wall of self realization,
Avoiding pity and misery,
Avoiding secrets and pairs of staring eyes,
Avoiding echoes of a guardian emotion,
Superior than my ,
I share some deadly venom,
Life is a game of heaven and hell,
I am a viper in disguise.

87. Poem 87

I bear the load of reputation
Miserable parts of me
Float on the clouds of
Peaceful poetry
Radiating hope and positivity .
I stand alone
In a blue gown , asking for a cure
Power fades away
And my face evaporates
Bringing back painful remembrance
Of love and grief .
A part of me
Looses all its flow
While a part dares to fight more
Like ashes after retaliation
Fight with the wind
And then secretly vanish away .
I owe so much to each and every word
Of each and every poem
Who made me realise and decipher
The reputation of life .

88. Poem 88

The way I want to rise up
Along with my female mates
The way sun comes up
After a havoc day .

89. Poem 89

There is no justification
To depression .
A wilted leaf
Hangs lifelessly on the branch
Without any motive or juice .
It is like a room you can't escape
A closed room without windows or doors
And familiar faces .
You are in a million and yet alone .
Depression is a struggle
A chaos inside of you .
A deadly phase where you loose
And really ,
Depression should never be a good friend !
Or can it be ?

90. Poem 90

She is running and chasing Hiraeth
Maa , papa and whom not
Love and care
Wisdom and togetherness
She craves hope .
She is a woman ,a basic one
With tiny aspirations
And her world is small enough
To fit in the pocket of jeans
Where all her fantasies
Escape this cruel place .
She saturates her will
With ink and paints
And rests her forehead
In the lap of books
She got no friends
No one to share
All what she is going through .
Literature and art
are the cause Of her euphoria
She is a seeker
And someone weaker

Someone with a puny heart .